CW00557325

Acknowledgements

Thanks to the following people and organisations for their kind permission to use copyright material in this book: The National Trust; David Yardley, A World in Miniature; Andrew Currie and Bonhams; Andrew Meek, Hobbies; TopToise; Barbara Andrews; City of Edinburgh Council; Peter and Kate, Herdwick Landscapes; Lauren George; Christine Jaeger; Oliver Mustoe-Playfair, Dolls House Emporium; Diane Pearson; Nadia Michaux; Rebecca Micallef; Sheri Followay; Gale Elena and Andrew Bantock; Val Lennie; Jane Wright; Jane Harrop; Tickhill Dollshouse Courses; Sarah and Geoffrey Walkley; Heather Drinkwater; Alexa and Rowan Dewar; Fay Zerbolio; Lundby; The Jewish Museum, London; Glasgow Museums Collection.

Thanks also to Paul, Spike and Ellie – my long-suffering family – for their patience when holidays and days out turned into hunts for dolls' house museums, or visits to dolls' house collectors' homes, dolls' house shops and fairs!

Every attempt has been made to seek permission for copyright material used in this book. However, if we have inadvertently used copyright material without permission/acknowledgement we apologise and will make the necessary correction at the first opportunity.

About the Author

Moi Ali has written many books for leading publishers in her professional field of marketing and communications. However, she is also passionate about dolls' houses and owns a large collection of houses, room boxes and miniature furniture. She has contributed features to all three of the UK dolls' house magazines over many years. She now writes exclusively for *Dolls' House and Miniature Scene Magazine* on a freelance basis. She has a monthly column in the magazine and writes regular features on dolls' house makers and collectors.

DOLLS' HOUSES

A History and Collector's Guide

Moi Ali

AMBERLEY

First published 2016

Amberley Publishing
The Hill, Stroud
Gloucestershire, GL5 4EP

www.amberley-books.com

Copyright © Moi Ali, 2016

The right of Moi Ali to be identified as the Author
of this work has been asserted in accordance with
the Copyrights, Designs and Patents Act 1988.

ISBN 978 1 4456 5345 7 (print)
ISBN 978 1 4456 5346 4 (ebook)

All rights reserved. No part of this book may be
reprinted or reproduced or utilised in any form
or by any electronic, mechanical or other means,
now known or hereafter invented, including
photocopying and recording, or in any information
storage or retrieval system, without the permission
in writing from the Publishers.

British Library Cataloguing in Publication Data.
A catalogue record for this book is available from
the British Library.

Typesetting by Amberley Publishing.
Printed in the UK.

Contents

A Brief History of Dolls' Houses and Miniatures

The history of miniaturism goes right back to the days of the ancient pharaohs. Think little King Tut sitting with his mummy (the un-bandaged variety) alongside the Nile playing with his toy pyramid. A quaint image, but an inaccurate one.

Yes, it's a historical fact that miniature houses, complete with furniture, little wooden people (such as fishermen, farmers and servants), animals and even small boats were made in Egypt nearly 5000 years ago. Despite the best efforts of grave robbers, many examples of these clay houses have been found in ancient tombs. However, these miniature items were not playthings for children, adults or even pharaohs. It is believed that they were funerary items that were buried with people for their later use in the afterlife. Burial rituals were tremendously important in Ancient Egypt, not so much because they were obsessed with death, but because they believed in the afterlife.

Miniature granaries were also a feature of many a wealthy person's tomb, in the belief that they would secure a food supply in the afterlife. With the Nile being such a life-giver in this desert region, it is not surprising that tombs also contained miniature boats.

Collectors are unlikely to be able to afford a genuine Ancient Egyptian miniature – unless they have a very large wallet, as these ancient collectibles are very pricey and rare.

Baby Houses

We tend to think of dolls' houses as affordable playthings for young girls, not expensive trophies for grown men. However, the first dolls' houses were exactly that: status symbols for the aristocracy, rather as an Aston Martin might be today.

Duke Albrecht V of Bavaria commissioned the first recorded dolls' house back in 1557 – known as a 'baby' house, although it was not a house for babies or children, nor even a baby or small house. It was a miniaturised version of one of his grand ducal residences. With four storeys, a garden, stable, barn and dairy, it was positively palatial. Sadly this house, known as the Munich Baby House, was destroyed by fire in 1674.

Opinions are divided as to why these early miniature buildings were called baby houses. Some say that it is because they were baby or small versions of big houses. Others take the view that as dolls were known at that time as babies, a house for dolls would be known as a baby house.

Duke Albrecht started a fashion among the best families in the land for baby houses, and the trend spread well beyond the Bavarian boundary. Exquisite replica houses were commissioned from the finest craftsmen and put on display in pride of place in the grand mansions of Germany, Holland and Britain.

This modern German dolls' house looks very different to the early Bavarian 'baby' houses of the sixteenth century.

These bijou buildings were kitted out with miniature fine furnishings, paintings, porcelain, silverwares and everything else that could be found in a stately home at that time.

Aside from being beautiful objects in their own right, German baby houses served an educational purpose in the seventeenth and eighteenth centuries, teaching aristocratic girls and young women the basics of running a grand house and keeping servants.

Baby houses from the Netherlands were generally not what we would recognise today as dolls' houses. Dutch dolls' houses were effectively cabinets, and are referred to as 'cabinet houses' for that reason. Furnished miniature rooms were contained within the cabinet.

Early British dolls' houses were also in cabinet form, although by the eighteenth century we had adopted the German taste for a more architectural style of dolls' house. The earliest surviving British house, Ann Sharp's Baby House of around 1695, is privately owned and in the form of a cupboard rather than a house.

As the dolls' house originated in Bavaria, it is fitting that the world's earliest surviving dolls' house is on display in Bavaria. Dating to 1611, it is in the German National Museum in Nuremburg. Other early dolls' houses are also in that museum, including the Stromer House, dating to 1639, and two later seventeenth-century houses – the Kress House and the Baumler House. In the UK, a Nuremburg house dating to 1673 can be seen at the Victoria and Albert Museum of Childhood in London. Early Dutch houses can be seen in Utrecht (Petronella de la Court's cabinet house of around 1670) and in Amsterdam (Petronella Dunois' 1676 house).

Seventeenth-century dolls' houses rarely come onto the market, although genuine Georgian dolls' houses come up for sale occasionally (and there are a number of fine eighteenth-century houses on display in museums and stately homes).

Throstlenest House, a rare and important late Georgian oak dolls' house and stand, dating from 1760–1780, came up for sale at Bonhams in 2006, selling for £9,600. This dolls' house reflects the typical style of Georgian grand palatial houses, with its front entrance flanked by two columns and portico, with quoining to the central panel and sides. Its fourteen glazed oblong windows have moulded surrounds, sills and glazing bars. It sits on an original carved and painted stone effect arched wooden stand.

Collector Barbara Andrews commissioned
this cabinet house eleven years ago, inspired by
Petronella Dunois's dolls' house, dating from
1676 and now in the Rijksmuseum, Amsterdam.
(Petronella Oortman's dolls' house of around 1686 is
also at that museum.)

The interior of Barbara Andrews' modern cabinet
house shows a more conventional dolls' house
layout.

The rooms in Barbara Andrews' cabinet house
incorporate every architectural detail that one
would expect in a period dolls' house.

One of the most important eighteenth-century British dolls' houses, this Palladian mansion, with original furnishings, sits on an arcaded stand. It was made for Sarah Lethieullier (circa 1730) and is on display in the National Trust's Uppark House in West Sussex. The writer H. G. Wells played with the dolls' house as a boy, as his mother was housekeeper there. (National Trust Images/Nadia Mackenzie)

This dolls' house has been attributed to architect James Paine and cabinetmaker Thomas Chippendale (it is believed that Chippendale also made the miniature furniture). Made *c.* 1735 for the Winn family, it is on display at the National Trust's Nostell Priory – the Winn family seat. The fireplaces are from James Gibbs's Book of Architecture of 1728. (National Trust Images/Andreas von Einsiedel)

This genuine Georgian house, Thornlenest House, was bought in the 1950s and remained in the same family until it went up for auction at Bonhams in 2006.

Once on loan to the Museum of Childhood in London, this rare Palladian-style dolls' house of the 1730s was put up for auction in 2009 for an estimated price of between £15,000 and £25,000.

Remarkably similar in style is a slightly earlier grand Palladian mahogany English dolls' house, circa 1730–1740. It too has a central section, quoining to corners and a triangular pediment. The house was designed using the architectural manuals of the period and bears similarities to the work of John Wood the Elder, the architect of Queen Square in Bath. It is believed to be modelled on a house in Richmond, London.

Even if a Georgian dolls' house were to come on the market, it is unlikely that the average enthusiast would be able to afford it. An alternative is to build your own Georgian-style dolls' house using plans from a book, and authentic-looking classical plaster mouldings to add period details for a convincing Georgian feel.

Mass-Production

Dolls' houses enjoyed their heyday during the Victorian era. Think about the traditional nursery in any middle-class Victorian home, in which a rocking horse and a dolls' house would be centre stage.

This late Victorian wooden dolls' house is unusual in that it opens front and rear, and has windows in the rear of the house too.

Mass-production meant that, instead of having to employ a skilled carpenter to produce a bespoke miniature building, families could walk into a toy shop and buy a more affordable machine-made dolls' house. Hamley's iconic Regent Street toy shop opened in 1881, and all big towns and cities would have a toy store of some sort.

Of course, amateur-made dolls' houses continued to be made throughout the Victorian era. Many charming examples survive and they are sought for their naïve charm.

Four paper lithographed, mass-produced late Victorian dolls' houses, sold by Bonhams.

These pretty dolls' houses are typical of the mass-produced models available in toy shops in the late nineteenth and early twentieth centuries.

This English dolls' house, *c.* 1848, was probably built by a competent amateur rather than mass-produced or craftsman-made.

Some of the one-off dolls' houses made during this period were very sophisticated. The English early Victorian painted wooden dolls' house shown below, dating to the 1850s, has a beautifully recreated glazed greenhouse with wooden shelving, steps and removable roof. The flag post displays a flag bearing the family crest of Ann Loxdale, the little girl who originally owned the house. Her family had links to sugar and coffee plantations in the West Indies, and Aigburth was known as an area where slave-ship and plantation owners lived.

Dolls' houses could also be purchased via mail order, using the relatively new postal service. A newspaper advert from 1888, advertised Dimple Villa, 'A real doll's house for one shilling'. Postage and carriage for this flat-pack house would set you back another 4*d*!

The manufacturer of Dimple Villa was London-based Hinde's, who had a range of popular shilling toys. Hinde's advertised its shilling dolls' house as a 'quite wonderful toy for the money', being 'a most attractive double-fronted residence' with 'imitation red brick and stone facings, bay windows, green Venetian blinds'. We think of Victorian dolls' houses as a taste of nostalgia, but to the Victorians these houses were bang up-to-date. The shilling house had 'interior decoration all in the modern style. Dados, bright wallpapers &c.'

With a larger number of children owning dolls' houses, enterprising Victorians in the United Kingdom and abroad began making affordable miniature furniture, ornaments, china and utensils, drapery and soft furnishing. Many were made by small family businesses in Britain and Germany, and may have been produced as a cottage industry using exploited child labour. Homemade items were also incorporated, some crafted by doting parents and others by the girls who owned the dolls' houses. The average Victorian twelve-year-old girl was quite an accomplished needlewoman, well able to sew a small pair of curtains, make bedding and create a little tapestry rug.

Dolls' houses made in the Victorian era are still reasonably plentiful, albeit often quite expensive. Straddling the Victorian and Edwardian period was Art Nouveau. There are very few period Art Nouveau dolls' houses, although there are well-known reproductions. Scotland's take on Nouveau was spearheaded by Charles Rennie Mackintosh, and there are several quality Mackintosh-style houses. A mass-produced reproduction was made by Dolls House Emporium, although it was discontinued

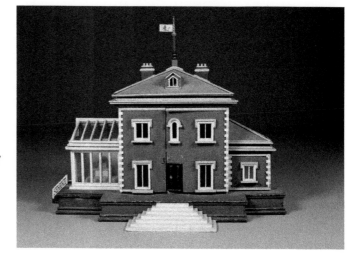

Made for the daughter of merchant George Henry Loxdale of Kingsland House, Aigburth, Liverpool, this dolls' house is believed to be a copy of the family home. She was still living in Kingsland in the 1881 census (aged thirty-two), with her widowed father and two sisters.

some years ago. The Mackintosh House made by Margaret and Michael Hartley (see below), and the miniature Mackintosh Ladies' Luncheon Room made by members of the North Glasgow Dolls' House Group, are in the collection of the Glasgow Museums, although they are not currently on display.

Glasgow Museums own four further Mackintosh 1:20-scale models, commissioned for their 1996 Mackintosh exhibition. Made by Brian Gallagher of BG Models Ltd, the one of Scotland Street School is on permanent display in the Scotland Street School Museum. The other three (of Hill House, the Willow Tea Rooms and Phase One of the Glasgow School of Art) are on permanent display in the Mackintosh Room at The Lighthouse in Glasgow. BG Models made another two 1:20-scale models of the Glasgow School of Art as completed in 1909: one of the whole building, the other of the library. These are in the Glasgow School of Art's own collection and often on display.

Left: This Mackintosh dolls' house is in storage as it is made from materials that are easily damaged by light and cannot be displayed for long periods. (CSG CIC Glasgow Museums Collection)

Below: This Mackintosh miniature furniture was made by Joan Rouch of TopToise Design in Scotland.

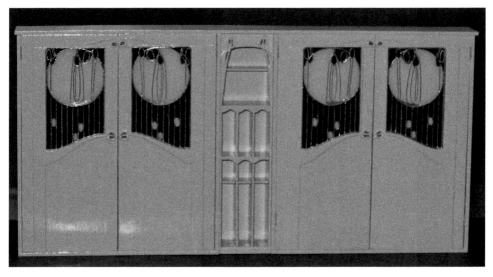

Edwardian dolls' houses are also rare, perhaps in part because the Edwardian era spanned a short time period, so fewer houses were made. The mother of all Edwardian/interwar dolls' houses – not to mention the mother of all dolls' houses, full stop! – is Queen Mary's. It was created for Queen Mary, consort to King George V, by the renowned architect Sir Edwin Lutyens between 1921 and 1924 – with electricity, running water and functioning lifts. It is filled with Doulton and Wedgwood porcelain, oil paintings by respected artists, crystal chandeliers and marble-topped giltwood tables, and a library of original books by prominent authors including Conan Doyle, Thomas Hardy, Rudyard Kipling and Sir James Barrie. (Virginia Woolf and George Bernard Shaw refused to write miniature books for the Queen.) Each of the tiny books has a bookplate drawn by E. H. Shepherd, illustrator of *Winnie the Pooh*.

Other Edwardian dolls' houses cannot claim such an illustrious history, but they are charming nonetheless. Both mass-produced and one-offs can be found in Edwardian style.

Made in the Edwardian era, this English painted wooden dolls' house reflects the architectural style of a typical middle-class Edwardian home.

The verandah adds charm to this Edwardian house.

Dating to 1906, this delightful Edwardian dolls' house is at the National Trust's Castle Drogo, Devon. It was made for Mary, elder daughter of Drogo owner Julius Drewe, by a carpenter at Wadhurst Hall (at that time, the young Mary's home). (National Trust Images/John Hammond)

If you are unable to find a genuine Edwardian dolls' house, commissioning an Edwardian-style house is an option. Some modern miniaturists, such as Chris Rouch of TopToise Designs, have a good understanding of period architecture and great attention to detail, enabling them to build dolls' houses with a very authentic appearance.

Twenty-first-century miniaturist Chris Rouch of TopToise Design made this delightful pair of Edwardian-style semi-detached dolls' houses as a special commission.

Selkirk-based Chris Rouch of TopToise made this Edwardian-style home, with authentic-looking leaded glass windows.

A more hands-on approach to securing an Edwardian-style villa is to build it yourself, using plans from the era. Hobbies sell plans based on those from their 1917 handbook. The original plans, which were given away in 1917, form the basis for the modernised Edwardian house below.

Miniaturist Jane Harrop has written a book containing plans for authentic-looking Edwardian and Arts and Crafts furniture, so you can kit out your house with appropriate furnishings. For inspiration, see the beautiful miniature Edwardian room at A World in Miniature in Carlisle.

This modern dolls' house can be built from plans sold by Hobbies. The original plans, upon which the house is based, date back to 1917 – the No. 93 Fretwork Special.

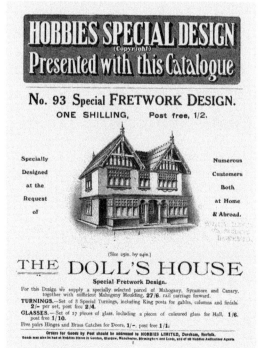

This 1917 Hobbies' catalogue cover shows the original Edwardian No. 93 Fretwork Special. It contains much more decorative detail than its modern version – such as shingle roof tiles, elaborate turnings and fretwork, pillars to the porch and multi-paned Edwardian windows.

Left: Talented miniaturist Jane Harrop has drawn up detailed instructions for how to make authentic-looking Edwardian dolls' house furniture, such as this bed, which is so typical of the era. They can be found in her book on Arts and Crafts and Edwardian furniture.

Below: This Edwardian-style room box at A World in Miniature is modern, but it captures the essence of the era with authentic recreations of classic Arts and Crafts pieces.

Even well into the twentieth century, mass-production did not lead to the extinction of homemade dolls' houses. Fathers and grandfathers continued to make bespoke little (and not so little) houses for their daughters and granddaughters – and still make them, to this day, in sheds and garages across the land. One father, Geoffrey Walkley, completed the dolls' house shown opposite (top) for his daughter in 2013 – thirty-five years after he started!

Some of these homemade dolls' houses tell a story of social history. One particular modernist style dolls' house, which is in the collection of the Jewish Museum in London, was made by Malcolm Libling, the son of an East End furniture maker, for his daughter Thelma. It is based on an actual house in the seaside town of Angmering-on-Sea. The dolls' house shown opposite (bottom) demonstrates the aspirations of the Jewish community who had grown up in the cramped streets and housing of London's East End. During the interwar period they started to build new communities in the suburbs, which offered more space and better housing. This dolls' house encapsulates the aspirations of a whole community.

Retired lawyer Geoffrey Walkley spent thirty-five years building this exquisite dolls' house for his daughter Sarah. It is based on the National Trust's Rainham Hall in Essex. Sarah was forty by the time she took possession in 2013 – but she says it was worth the wait.

Architect Tom Rutherford built this dolls' house in 1986 as a Christmas present for his six-year-old granddaughter, Rowan Dewar. It is an exact replica of her childhood home in Edinburgh.

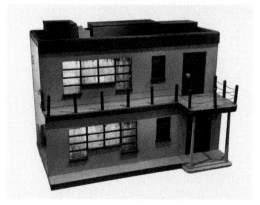

Thelma's House, courtesy of London's Jewish Museum.

One of Tri-ang's Ultra Modern range of dolls' houses, made around 1937. Tri-ang miniature houses reflected popular taste in domestic architecture. Although this Art Deco house is very collectable today, the geometric lines were not to everyone's taste at that time. Children (or perhaps their parents) preferred Tri-ang's more traditional cottages and houses, so few Ultra Moderns were produced – adding to the desirability of such models today. This one has altered doors. The originals were of planked chevron design.

The Art Deco house of the 1930s was striking for its angular departure from the more traditional and fussy Victorian and Edwardian styles. Streamlined houses in white, with the air of ocean liners, typified modern housing at that time. The clean lines synonymous with Deco style came to be reflected in both one-off bespoke dolls' houses and also mass-produced miniature houses such as the Number 53 by Tri-ang.

Deco-style dolls' houses can be commissioned today, although few makers specialise in that period. One miniature maker who loves Art Deco is Chris Rouch of TopToise Design, who has made several models.

Of more recent vintage is this miniaturised version of a real Art Deco house in Spalding, Lincolnshire. The 12th-scale dolls' house is by Chris Rouch of Selkirk-based TopToise Designs, which he runs with his wife Joan.

This 24th-scale model of
Usherwood, an Art Deco house
in Surrey, was built by TopToise.

This is a tiny 48th-scale Art
Deco house by Chris Rouch.

Another beautiful Art Deco
creation by Chris Rouch of
TopToise Designs.

From the 1930s to the 1960s, there was a trend for home-built houses – not *scratch*-built, but models constructed at home using either commercially available plans from leading companies such as Hobbies, or dolls' house kits.

Hobbies published an annual catalogue of tools and materials – the *Hobbies Handbook* – as well as a weekly magazine. Many hobbyists' crafts were covered, not just dolls' houses.

These Hobbies dolls' house kits date to the late 1960s.

This free plan for the 'chalet' dolls' house was included in the 1968 Hobbies *Annual*.

Hobbies also sold components such as doors and windows, which could be incorporated into homemade houses for a more professional finish. Up until the 1960s, dolls' houses were made from wood, sometimes with tin components such as windows.

By the 1960s and 1970s, plastic was being widely used in dolls' house production, and by the 1980s, MDF too – although quality dolls' houses have always been constructed from wood, and timber continues to be used today.

In the 1980s, there was a growing interest in fine miniatures among adults. Dolls' house collecting (antique, vintage and new) became an increasingly popular adult pursuit. Talented makers such as Mulvany and Rogers were (and continue to be) much in demand for their exquisite miniature renditions of fine period homes.

Things have come full circle: baby houses were once expensive 'toys' for adults in the sixteenth and seventeenth centuries, and again today grown-ups are spending big money commissioning bespoke model houses, or collecting expensive antique ones. Yes, children will always enjoy playing with toy houses, but the dolls' house hobby is now a very grown-up one, which has finally come of age.

This handmade house is based on a Hobbies' plan and uses a tin door, most likely purchased from Hobbies but made by Romside.

Tin doors and windows typified early Hobbies houses – and some had real glass in the windows – but by 1968 this 'chalet' dolls' house had plastic components.

Jenny's Home range, made by Rovex Industries and sold, among others, by Hobbies, was plastic. Plastic modular rooms could be joined to create unique buildings, and furnished with plastic furniture.

Expensive miniatures such as this Mulvany and Rogers Grand Dining Room at A World in Miniature, Carlisle, show that this hobby at the top-end requires a salary rather than pocket money! The focal point of this miniature masterpiece is a grand fireplace, supported by caryatids and flanked by fitted alcoves containing a collection of precious miniature glass and ceramics. A mahogany dining table with silverware, fine glassware and cutlery, is lit by a magnificent silver chandelier with real wax candles.

Principal Dolls' House Manufacturers

Since the Victorian era, when dolls' houses began to be mass-produced, there have been many manufacturers in the UK, Europe and the United States. Some were small or short-lived companies; others large and enduring. There have also been relatively recent start-up companies. It is impossible to list all of them in this small guide, but the following gives an indication of the wide range of companies past and present.

Lundby

Lundby was established in 1945 by Axel and Grete Thomsen, who lived in the neighbourhood of Lundby in Gothenburg. Grete built a dolls' house and furniture for her niece: she and her friends loved it so much that Axel considered setting up a dolls' house business. Two years later a leading Swedish department store placed the first order and the couple invested the advance payment in new tools. The first dolls' house factory opened the following year. Lundby continues in business, making the Småland (which has changed little over the years) and the Stockholm, a more modern dolls' house. Both are modular, allowing various combinations. Although their houses are made for children, vintage Lundby homes and furniture have become popular with adult collectors.

This 1981 Lundby house is owned by collector Diane Pearson. It shows how components could be stacked to create a range of configurations. The furniture here dates mainly to the 1970s.

A twenty-first-century Småland by Lundby, not hugely different from earlier versions.

Lundby's architect-designed twenty-first-century Stockholm dolls' house.

Lines and Tri-ang

George and Joseph Lines established G. & J. Lines Ltd in the nineteenth century, making wooden toys, and, by the end of the century, quality dolls' houses too.

Joseph Lines' three sons wanted to produce more modern designs, which reflected popular taste in twentieth-century domestic architecture and interiors. They established their own company, Lines Bros Ltd, in 1919. Manufacturing under the Triangtois trade name, this was later changed to Tri-ang. Three lines make a triangle, and three Lines brothers formed Tri-ang!

Tri-ang produced an extensive range of dolls' houses, including thatched cottages, country houses, bungalows, and even, by the 1930s, cutting-edge geometric modern dolls' houses in the Art Deco style. The wallpapers used by Tri-ang were specially printed scaled-down versions of contemporary designs.

During the Second World War, the company made machine guns – real ones, not toys. It was not uncommon for factories to be requisitioned by the State for the war effort.

Tri-ang's Tudor dolls' houses proved to be most popular with buyers, which is why they remained in production for several decades.

This large painted wooden G. & J. Lines house dates to *c.* 1910 and sold at Bonhams for £1,800 in 2011.

The Tri-ang logo.

This Tri-ang 61, belonging to collector Diane Pearson, is one of the company's popular mock-Tudor designs, which was in production from 1949 to 1958.

This Tri-ang 50 remains desirable and is collected to this day.

Mock-Tudor Tri-ang 'Stockbroker' house from the 1930s, in the collection of the Museum of Childhood, Edinburgh. This one is missing its chimneys. The fancy end chimney is often missing from this model, along with the front steps, as they were not attached to the house and frequently became separated from it.

Tri-ang enthusiasts have a particular fondness for the Princess Elizabeth dolls' house, modelled on Y Bwythn Bach, or the Little House. The real Y Bwythn Bach, in the grounds of Windsor's Royal Lodge, was built, furnished and decorated by Welsh craftsmen and presented to the Queen (then Princess Elizabeth) on her sixth birthday in 1932. It is 24 feet long, 8 feet deep and contains rooms just 5 feet high. Originally it had heat, light, running water, gas, a working fridge, a bathroom with heated towel rail and a telephone – at a time when many real homes lacked these facilities. Fit for a queen, in fact. Princess Beatrice recently refurbished the royal Wendy house. The dolls' house came in two sizes, the larger having a garage too.

Perhaps the most coveted Tri-ang dolls' house of all time is the bespoke model made at the Lines Brothers' Merton factory in around 1933 for Henrietta Katherine Peggy Lines, the eldest daughter of joint founder and chairman of Lines Brothers, Walter Lines. (Her sister Gillian also had a dolls' house made by the factory). Peggy's house – based on Leigh Place, her lavish childhood home in Surrey – is a more elaborate version of the Mayflower series of dolls' houses made by Lines/Tri-ang from 1927. Peggy went on to become Chairman of Hamleys, the famous toy store. She gave her dolls' house to a nephew in the early 1990s, as she had no children of her own. It was sold by Bonhams in 2011 for £2,400 and is now on display at the Museum of Childhood in Bethnal Green, London.

Tri-ang went into receivership and closed in 1971.

Tri-ang Princess Elizabeth, from the Museum of Childhood, Edinburgh, launched in 1939 and was in production until 1957. The house is just 24 inches x 30 inches x 17 inches.

This unique and important painted wooden dolls' house, the Peggy Lines House, has a separate garage with chauffeur's quarters.

Hobbies of Dereham, Hobby's and Handicraft

Two suppliers of dolls' house paraphernalia go by very similar names: Hobbies and Hobby, publishers of *Hobby's Annuals*. Both sell dolls' house supplies, and to add to the confusion, Hobby also sell various Hobbies' designs from the 1950s and 1960s, which it bought when the original Hobbies went out of business many years ago.

Hobbies has been supplying model-makers and miniaturists since the nineteenth century. The famous *Hobbies Weekly* was first published in 1895. Hobbies' *Annual* dates to 1881 and remains popular today.

John Skinner set up Hobbies in Norfolk, but emigrated to South Africa in 1902. His brother Frank worked there, but left the company to establish rival firm Handicrafts, poaching key staff including Hobbies' chief designer. He copied the Hobbies mailing list and sent customers rival publicity materials. In 1907, Hobbies took legal action and won damages.

Hobbies continued publishing *Hobbies Weekly* and their *Annual* throughout the First World War. During the Second World War, Hobbies manufactured components for aircraft, as well as continuing with their normal business.

The charming illustrations in old Hobbies magazines and catalogues are collected in their own right by vintage dolls' house enthusiasts, who like to own original images and adverts for their model of Hobbies house.

LARGE TUDOR DOLL'S HOUSE

No. 237 Special
2 ft. wide. 2 ft. high. 16 ins. deep.
An attractive model of a typical half-
timbered Tudor House. Access is pro-
vided to the spacious interior by a
double-door hinged front. The design
sheet contains patterns of parts, including staircase, and details for building.
The kit of material contains panels of
plywood the correct thickness required
for all parts, material for staircase, sheets
of card for the roof, set of windows and
doors in painted metal ready for fixing,
four metal fireplaces and sufficient brick,
tile, floor and wallpaper. The whole kit
(No. 237 Special) ready to cut out and
build, supplied for 89/6. Carriage Paid
from Dereham (United Kingdom only).
Design & Instructions, apart from Kit, 3/-

**Dolls' Houses
to Build**

The company published plans for miniature versions of contemporary houses. It wasn't until the 1950s that Hobbies began to look to older styles of architecture, producing a Georgian-style dolls' house, an Old Curiosity Shop, and a galleried coaching inn. Even so, contemporary designs were still produced, such as – in the 1960s – the Royal Dolls' House with picture windows; the flat-roofed Celebrity bungalow with car port; the Dreamhome with large sliding patio doors; and the Twinplay Motel with car park, petrol pumps and helipad – all embodying classic sixties architectural style.

The last dolls' house designed by Hobbies before the original company closed was the Chalet, a modern house with a typical 1960s downstairs layout comprising lounge and dining alcove. (It can still be bought today from Hobby.)

Hobbies followed furniture trends, issuing plans for Art Deco furniture sets in the 1930s. However, arch-rival Handicrafts were ahead of them in many respects, selling both dolls' house electrical lighting systems, and also furniture, many years before Hobbies.

Once there were ten Hobbies shops across the UK and, in 1961, the company had 500 staff. It was taken over in 1964 by catalogue empire Great Universal Stores, who sold the shops and closed the business. *Hobbies Weekly* ceased publication in 1965, although the *Annual* continued production. In 1968 the company was wound up and its assets sold.

Former Hobbies' employee, Ivan Stroulger, used his redundancy money to establish the Dereham Handicraft Company, making kits for dolls' houses from his garden shed.

DOLL'S GARAGE
No. 2766

Although this small garage model is designed to the same proportion as the doll's house (237 Special), to form a companion to that house, it can be built as an independent piece of work suitable for any small cars or motor vehicles. It is 10 ins. long by 7½ ins. wide and its metal doors open to a width of 4 ins. to allow a good-sized model inside.

PAINTING OUTFIT	Kit of design, card for roof, panels of plywood, metal windows and double doors,
For painting these models we supply a Painting Outfit of six colours. See page 115.	brick paper and roof paper, 15/9, including Tax. *Design separately,* **8d.**

Hobbies made a wide range of kits for miniature buildings, including this charming garage.

Ivan went into partnership with a Hobbies colleague, setting up Hobby Trends. In 1975, Ivan formed Hobbies and Handicrafts (Dereham) Ltd. In 1978, now in his sixties, he acquired the Hobbies name, trademark, patents and copyright. His sons joined him at the company and, in 1993, set up the Hobbies Museum in Dereham.

Ivan began designing dolls' houses, including a windmill dolls' house and gypsy caravan dolls' house. Some of his designs were sold through rival company Hobby's. In the 1970s, Hobby's bought the original Hobbies' dolls' house designs from the 1950s and 1960s. They are still on sale today. One of the original designs, the No. 237 Special Large Tudor doll's house, has been modified by Hobby's and renamed the Tudor Doll's House.

In 2005, Andrew Meek and his wife Caroline bought the company, the museum's contents and the Hobbies' design archive.

Amersham Toy Company

This Chesham-based company was established in 1908 by German toymaker, Joseph Eisenmann. It started out making dolls, then teddies too. Son-in-law Leon Rees inherited the business in 1919. Production diversified into wooden dolls' houses and

This Amersham Uplands dates to the 1950s. Amersham tin windows are unique to that company.

Amersham dolls' houses came with card labels with a foil edge, tin-plate plaques or paper logos. They are difficult to date, but it is believed that the tin plate indicates an older house; card labels are mid-period; and paper labels were used until the company ceased making dolls' houses in around 1953.

furniture. Many of the houses designed by the company look like the local inter-war 'Met' houses constructed by the Metropolitan Railway Country Estates Ltd.

Barton

A. Barton & Co. (Toys) Ltd began trading in 1945, immediately after the Second World War. Their collection of 16th-scale items included plaster fireplaces, wooden 'wireless' radios, grandfather clocks, electric 'bar' fires and old 'box' televisions in cabinets. In the mid-1950s they brought out a 16th-scale dolls' house, available ready-built and as a kit. In 1975 the company introduced the successful plastic Caroline's Home range. Many of the designs made by Barton in the 1970s bore an uncanny resemblance to Swedish company Lundby's items. In 1984, Barton was bought by Lundby.

This Barton plastic bathroom suite probably dates to the 1970s.

Moritz Gottschalk

From 1873 German manufacturer Moritz Gottschalk made dolls' houses, which were exported to Britain, France, the Netherlands, Scandinavia and America. From around 1880 until 1910, the roofs were a distinctive blue, but later models usually had a red roof. Collectors struggled to identify their Gottschalk dolls' houses, until the original factory illustrations of Gottschalk catalogues for 1892–1931 surfaced. After the Second World War, Gottschalk was in the eastern zone of occupied Germany, yet it restarted production in 1947. During the following years, the company made dolls' houses in the style of the time, with typical 1950s and 1960s designs on offer. In 1972, all remaining private businesses in the German Democratic Republic were nationalised and Gottschalk was merged within nationally owned VERO. For a few years the company continued to build toy parts in its factory in Marienberg, before closure.

This blue-roofed Gottschalk dolls' house was made for the French market. It has a decorative red-brick and grey lithographed exterior.

A Moritz Gottschalk paper lithographed red-brick model 3735 blue-roofed dolls' house (right) and a Gottschalk model 3738 (left), with lithographed exterior, metal balcony, four glazed windows and blue roof.

A Gottschalk model 3185 red-roofed cream-painted wooden dolls' house with portico with decorative lattice, small veranda to side entrance and six glazed windows, with painted window bars and a further two stencilled windows to each side. Generally a red roof indicates a later house.

Inside the Moritz Gottschalk 3185 red-roof.

Bliss

A favourite among American collectors is Bliss. The R. Bliss Manufacturing Company was established by Rufus Bliss in Rhode Island in 1832 and began making dolls' houses around 1880. As with many dolls' houses of the era, Bliss houses were wooden structures covered with lithograph-printed paper. Most of their houses are easy to identify, as they have the name 'Bliss' lithographed on them.

Silber & Fleming

Shallow dolls' houses with plain sides and a brickwork front, akin to a terraced house, are known as 'box back' houses. Many were made by anonymous makers (and thus bear no maker's mark) in the second half of the nineteenth century and into the twentieth. Box back houses could be bought in leading department stores of Victorian London,

This Silber & Fleming painted wooden dolls' house, circa 1890, has a sandstone and red-brick façade and stands on a green base. It was sold by Bonhams.

A wooden Silber & Fleming dolls' house, circa 1880, with white lower level and red-brick paper above.

such as Silber & Fleming. Some were British-made; others imported from Germany. It is believed that Silber & Fleming did not make their own houses, although these box back houses are often referred to as Silber & Fleming-type houses.

Dolls House Emporium

Founded in 1979 by Jackie Lee and her then-husband Adam Purser, the Dolls House Emporium's (DHE) original range comprised three 24th-scale kits, sold mail order from their home. The couple got their first premises in 1983, in Derbyshire. DHE grew to have a manufacturing workshop, warehousing, offices and shop – and a wide range of dolls' houses, kits, furniture and accessories. By 1992 the manufacturing of the dolls' houses was sub-contracted, and the company was supplying retailers as well as selling direct to the public. An advert from 1996 boasted a forty-eight-page full-colour catalogue. In 2010 DHE supplied props for the 20th Century Fox film, *Gulliver's Travels*. The company remained family-owned until 2013, when internet retailer MyHobbyStore bought the business – although Amy Purser, the founders' daughter, stayed on and worked for the new owners for a while. DHE have produced many popular and distinctive houses over the years, including models based on the design styles of key architects such as Lutyens and Mackintosh. These are now retired and its extensive range of houses now includes a swanky Art Deco Malibu Beach House, the classical Georgian Grosvenor Hall and medieval Cumberland Castle kit, as well as other traditional dolls' houses and smaller 12th-scale buildings such as a gazebo, garage and pavilion.

DHE's resin Butterfly Cottage is very rare, as it was only made for a year between September 2000 and August 2001. It is handmade and hand-painted.

This is one of the rarest DHE dolls' houses, Tudor Manor, built in 1979 by founders Adam Purser and Jackie Lee. It is one of their first two dolls' house models and is in the collection of Rebecca Micallef.

The chimney on this DHE model is handmade by founder Adam Purser; it has been numbered and bears the initials TM, possibly for Tudor Manor (the name of the house) or, more likely, Tudor Models (the name of the company at the outset). The DHE founders' daughter, Amy, was given an identical house.

This DHE Retreat, in need of renovation, is in my own collection. It is one of the smaller kits in their range.

This discontinued DHE house, from my collection, dates to around 2001.

Real Good Toys

American company Real Good Toys has been in business in Vermont since 1972, making quality dolls' house kits using carefully hand-crafted parts. The company says that its dolls' houses have been under the White House Christmas tree, featured on Hollywood television and film sets, and owned by celebrities. Their kits have been stocked by the Smithsonian Gift Shop (the equivalent of our V&A) and the Abraham Lincoln Presidential Museum, as well as top-notch toy stores such as F.A.O. Schwarz. Their models include a Vermont farmhouse, a beachside bungalow and an Adirondack log cabin.

There are many contemporary and vintage dolls' house furniture manufacturers too, such as Dol-Toi, Brimtoy, Pit-A-Pat, Kleeware, Bespaq and JiaYi … but that's the subject of a whole book in its own right!

This impressive wooden parquetry dolls' house was made around the 1860s–80s. It is clearly not a mass-produced item by a known maker, but a one-off specially built for someone very lucky. The façade and roof have been finished in geometric parquetry using specimen woods including walnut, sycamore, black walnut, satinwood, mahogany and tulip wood.

Antique and vintage dolls' house furniture is a specialist area in its own right.

If you don't have the expertise to collect old furniture, there's always new furniture in period styles, such as this pretty gilt sofa by Chinese maker JiaYi.

Starting or Extending a Collection

Most people just adore miniature things! Perhaps the appeal lies in their small scale, or that fact that a miniature world is one that can be controlled by the adult – it can be perfect and ordered; a slice of nostalgia; a memory of childhood; a diminutive version of the kind of home you could never afford in full-size. The hobby is one that appeals to architecture fans, students of history, interior design enthusiasts, creative handcrafters, sticklers for detail – in short, a wide range of people.

If you're new to the dolls' house hobby and would like to start a collection – or you have a collection already but you wish to extend into new areas of collecting – there are a various considerations. What scale should you major on? Vintage, antique or new dolls' houses? Kits or ready-made buildings? Houses, or other miniature scenes? Anyone unsure where to start should consider joining a dolls' house club. Clubs across the UK comprise friendly and helpful enthusiasts who are invariably happy to offer advice and guidance to newbies.

Some dolls' houses are so perfect in scale, architectural features and historical detail that, in photographic form, it can be hard to believe that they are models. This 12th-scale room is on display at A World in Miniature.

Dolls' house clubs are usually happy to accept members with all skill levels. They are a great place to learn from those who have been in the hobby for many years.

Scale

If you are about to take your first step into this fascinating hobby, begin by considering what scale you wish to collect.

The two most common scales are 12th and 24th. Most popular is 12th scale (sometimes written 1:12 or 1/12), where one inch represents an imperial 'foot' (12 inches).

In 24th scale, each half-inch translates to a foot. In other words, it is half the size of the standard 12th scale. Growing in popularity is 48th scale (1:48), where a quarter-of-an-inch represents one foot. For that reason it's often known as quarter scale. A five-foot tall figure in real life would be 5 inches in 12th scale, but just one-and-a-quarter inches in quarter scale.

Other scales are available too. There is 6th scale, which is enormous. The 6th-scale house shown on page 43, built from a kit by American company Real Good Toys, is almost five feet tall and made from cabinet grade plywood, unlike the MDF used in many dolls' house kits.

There's also 16th scale (don't be confused but it can be referred to as three-quarters or 18th scale – or 1:18 – because three-quarters of an inch represents a foot). It is sometimes known as 'Lundby Scale' after the famous 16th-scale Swedish dolls' house manufacturer.

Miniature settles in 12th, 24th and 48th scales show just how different the three most popular scales are.

This 12th-scale Victoria House is in my own collection and is a birch plywood house made by Anglesey. The company no longer exists.

The pound coin helps illustrate how tiny quarter scale is in this Petite Property kit house personalised by Gale Elena Bantock.

Again a pound coin gives a reference point to help understand the small scale of 1:48 models. This is a kit house by Jane Harrop.

The pound coin here shows how minuscule dolls' house furnishings are in quarter scale. These items are kits by Jane Harrop.

1/6 scale is the largest commercially available scale, although very few makers produce in this large scale.

Pros and Cons of Scales

There are benefits and drawbacks with all scales, so consider the pros and cons carefully before making a purchase.

Quarter scale takes up very little display space so you can have a huge collection without needing to live in a mansion. It also occupies very little storage space – your materials and work-in-progress can fit into a drawer or small cupboard, which is an important consideration for someone without a workshop or studio who wishes to work on kits. The scale's tiny footprint means that it's easy to find a suitable place to display a house or another building, such as on a narrow shelf or small table. The diminutive scale is really cute. Buildings are easily portable – meaning you can take them to display at events or to work on at dolls' house clubs or even on holiday. Buildings are lightweight and easy to lift for dusting and cleaning. There is not as much available in 48th scale (a drawback), so collectors are sometimes forced to make items themselves, although this does mean that the hobby is cheaper (a definite plus point). It also makes 48th-scale buildings more individual. Quarter-scale enthusiasts say that the scale is not about exact replication, so you can cut corners and create the illusion. For instance, a chest of drawers doesn't need separate drawers, making it easier.

The drawback with quarter scale is that it is so small, making it a very fiddly scale to work with. Good eyesight and/or good magnification are essential. It's a different concept to larger scales, involving illusion rather than replication, so it can be difficult for those used to working with larger scales to adjust. There are fewer suppliers at this scale, so less choice is available. As many things will have to be handmade, with no ready-made alternatives, some skill is required. Really tiny items, like a button or a sweetie, are impossible to make at such a small scale. Enthusiasts create the illusion by using a tiny dot or speck of glitter for buttons. It is a relatively modern scale and few antique and vintage models can be found in 48th scale.

This 48th-scale model by Herdwick Landscapes is very compact due to its small scale, making it ideal to display in a smaller home.

Even quite large houses are generally small models when translated into 48th scale. This Tabitha Twitchit dolls' house shop is made by Herdwick Landscapes.

This is a recreation of enthusiast Heather Drinkwater's own home in 48th scale. The full-sized version is a Georgian Listed Building. She made her mini replica using an Orchard House kit from Petite Properties and two of their Halfpenny House kits. Despite being in her seventies, she does not find such a small scale too much of a challenge to her eyesight.

This charming cottage by Heather Drinkwater is tiny, and furnishing such a small property can be a challenge. Much has to be homemade.

Half-inch scale is a good compromise scale. It's not as tiny as quarter scale, with all of the attendant problems of working with something so minuscule; at the same time, it's not as large and bulky as 12th scale. A good range of 24th-scale kits, ready-built houses and furniture can be found in shops, at fairs and online.

12th scale is often the preferred choice and, as a result, there is much more choice available – kits, ready-builts, antique houses and vintage properties. It is an easy scale with which to work, as it is not too small. However, a typical three-bedroomed house will take up quite a lot of space, so a collector may need to limit the number of houses they own.

A small number of collectors like 6th scale, but its downside is that it is huge. A completed house is enormous and will dominate a room. There is also a lack of choice when it comes to scale furniture and accessories. Few manufacturers make anything at 6th scale, so choice is limited.

Some homemade dolls' houses – particularly the older ones that were built without plans – are not built to any of the standard scales. This can pose problems if you wish to furnish your dolls' house using ready-made items, as they may look out-of-scale in your house.

A 24th-scale building, such as this quaint thatched cottage, is a good compromise scale, being neither too large nor too small.

Even this relatively small 12th-scale shop, part of my own collection, is quite large. It is just one room wide/deep, yet it is still 15 inches wide by 19 inches deep by 32 inches tall. Obviously a house with more rooms per floor will occupy a much larger footprint.

A fine wooden dolls' house, English, *c.* 1880. It is not unusual for dolls' houses of this period not to be built to a recognised scale, such as 12th or 24th. This can be problematic if you wish to furnish a homemade antique dolls' house with furniture of the appropriate scale.

Antique, Vintage or Modern

Antique dolls' houses are those aged 100 years or more. Such houses are rare and the older and rarer they are, the pricier they will be. Look out for houses that are in as near to original condition as possible, with original wall, floor, façade and roof papers; original doors, windows and window coverings, and fireplaces and ranges.

You may need deep pockets if you wish to collect antique houses, although some of the mass-produced models may be more affordable – and there are still bargains to be had at some provincial auction houses' general sales.

Remember to factor in the cost of insuring expensive antiques. You will need some expertise or advice if you are investing in costly collectibles, and it is wise to buy from reputable dealers or auction houses. An advantage of buying antique houses is that they sometimes come ready or partially furnished, and this can represent good value. However, some collectors like to buy unfurnished houses so that they can have fun tracking down authentic period pieces of furniture.

If you intend to build up a collection of antique dolls' houses, consider how you will conserve these potentially fragile artefacts. Think carefully about where and how they will be displayed. Environmental factors such as central heating, air-conditioning, bright sunlight, and extreme temperature changes such as those found in conservatories, can cause damage. Any dolls' house will be a guaranteed child-magnet, so keep anything financially valuable or sentimentally precious out of reach of little fingers – for your benefit and theirs (you don't want Junior rushed off to A&E with a miniature candlestick stuffed up his nose, in his ear or stuck in his throat!)

While there are many downsides to collecting antique houses, they are often very beautiful and they tend to hold their value. Wise purchases may even appreciate in value, representing a very good investment that brings more joy than stocks and shares ever could!

Vintage houses can be a good compromise for those who cannot afford antique, but have an aversion to a modern house. They may be shed-built creations constructed by amateurs, or mass-produced houses by leading companies such as Tri-ang and Lundby.

Look out for original features inside and out. This mid-nineteenth century house has original wall paint, floor papers and fireplaces.

It is clear here that the wallpaper is not original to the house, which dates to 1890. Repapering the house, probably in the 1960s, has affected its value.

These genuine Georgian fireplaces are valuable in their own right, but they came as part of the original fittings and fixtures from a Georgian dolls' house sold at auction, Throstlenest House.

From the late Victorian era and for decades afterwards, mass-produced dolls' houses were often covered with lithographed paper brickwork, roof tiles, doors and window detailing.

These dolls' houses have paper lithographed
exteriors, including lithographed window boxes.

Lithographed windows give the appearance of
window apertures.

Lithograph-printed windows and doors suggest
that these were cheaper dolls' houses when new, as
it would have been more labour-intensive to cut
apertures and to fit doors and windows.

This English three-storey painted wooden town house,
c. 1880, has a paper red-brick effect façade, with painted sides
and base. It was sold by Bonhams.

Inside, all six rooms have papered and painted walls and flooring and five have built-in fireplaces with soft metal hearths. The kitchen has a large stove. The house was sold fully furnished with good period furniture and accessories.

This 1875 painted wooden dolls' house was sold by Bonhams and is crammed full of unusual period furniture and accessories, including: a painted chair, tin-plate watering cans, bucket, cooking utensils, pots, rosewood bureau, desk, settee, chairs, gilt framed mirror, portrait, parrot on stand, tin-plate scroll-end bed with canopy, cot, rosewood wall cabinet, ornaments including flowers under glass domes, candle holders and even glasses.

This fine early English dolls' house, with polished wood exterior on a painted green wooden base, dates to the mid-nineteenth-century and was sold by Bonhams. It is sensible to use a reputable auction house if investing in expensive antique dolls' houses.

This painted, stone-effect double-fronted English wooden house, *c.* 1880s, was sold by Bonhams with early furniture, including painted tin dining room suite (oval table, four chairs, chaise longue and sideboard); other painted tin-plate including fireplace, cot, upright piano, wardrobe, drawers, kitchen stove, and a bath; also a red velvet upholstered chaise longue, tables and chairs. A house with its original contents is rare.

This vintage dolls' house, a Hobbies Fretwork design No. 237 special Tudor dolls' house, was purchased on eBay. The new owner, Jane Wright, intends to recreate her childhood home in miniature.

Dolls' houses from the 1950s, 1960s and 1970s are still widely available, although prices are rising as collectors recognise their growing appeal. The 1950s–70s is the era when many of today's collectors were growing up. Some choose to recreate their former family home in miniature, reliving memories of yesteryear; or to obtain a replica of their childhood dolls' house. It can be fun filling a vintage house with furniture you remember as a kid – the Danish teak sideboard, or the purple flock wallpaper! While vintage houses are generally more affordable than antique ones, they can sometimes be in a poor condition, play-worn, or suffering the effects of storage in damp outhouses and cold attics.

A brand new dolls' house is the safe option, and often the first choice for someone starting out in the hobby. A vast array of houses can be found, in many scales and designs, from Tudor and Georgian styles to Art Deco, 1930s and contemporary.

This modern shop is decorated in a nostalgic style. It is made from birch plywood and was designed by (the now defunct) Anglesey as a series of room boxes that sat one upon the other, with a shop room box at the bottom, an attic room box at the top, and any number of rooms stacked on the floors in between. It was very versatile as it could be added to over time.

Kit or Ready-Built

If you want a new house, choose either a ready-built structure, or a kit. Houses may come decorated, lit (electrified for lighting), and thus ready to receive furniture; or unpainted, undecorated and un-electrified. The state of readiness will be reflected in the price you pay.

Kits are cheaper than the equivalent ready-built houses. A kit will be flat-packed and ready to be assembled, and should come with instructions and sometimes glue too. Some manufacturers supply kits that are already painted, but most will be unpainted. Major components will usually be made from MDF (medium density fibreboard), although doors may be timber and windows plastic. Although a kit needs to be assembled, which takes some practical ability, most are relatively easy to put together, have been carefully designed with amateur home-assembly in mind, and require minimal tools and materials (usually nothing more than sandpaper, tape, glue, a hammer and screwdriver). Kits are usually made using laser-cutters or CNC milling machines, which cut very precisely for a good, snug fit using glue and sometimes panel pins too.

Beware when buying a kit, as not all kits include basic features such as internal doors, balustrades and sometimes even stairs. Be sure to check what is included in your kit, and to budget for finishing touches such as skirting boards, fireplaces, plaster ceiling roses, door handles, chimneys and chimney pots – as few kits will contain these. Paint a kit prior to assembly, as it is much harder to access the various tight little nooks and crannies once it has been put together.

Kits can be personalised externally with the addition of architectural features such as roughcast plaster finishes, fake brickwork, roof slates, leadwork on the roof, weather vanes and so on. Internally, too, added features such as chimney breasts and mock beams create a more individual house. You can also add these personalisations to a ready-built house.

This now-discontinued Dolls House Emporium 'Mountford' home is new, although it is in a period 1930s style. The company also made Fairfax, a larger version.

Kits usually comprise precision-cut MDF components, complete with instructions. This kit, a Stratford Bakery Kit from Dolls House Emporium, arrived with a wealth of extras, such as door handles and leaded windows.

This Stratford Bakery kit from Dolls House Emporium looks very realistic when finished. I added roof tiles and other extra details to create additional olde worlde charm to the kit.

This Morcott House kit from Barbara's Mouldings was my first ever kit some years ago, assembled for my daughter. It may have been more sensible to start small!

Kits can be improved with the addition of extra features. Here, I added roof tiles (made from a vinyl floor tile), a chimney stack, terracotta chimney pots and ridge tiles, and a laser-cut weather vane made from a Dutch kit.

Fake brickwork created using a stencil and brick compound adds a bespoke effect to a kit-built house.

The addition of a fake rear wall, plus fireplace, wood-panelled walls and a flagstone-effect floor add a bespoke look to this kit house.

Another option is to make your own dolls' house. Patterns and plans are available in books and specialist magazines, or can be purchased as stand-alone plans online. You can also design and make your dolls' house from your own plans, if you are skilled at designing, producing technical drawings, and carpentry. Courses are also available, including dolls' house holidays, where dolls' houses and other models can be created under the supervision of experts. It's a good way to tackle a model in a safe environment and to gain new skills – even for quite experienced miniaturists.

Even if you're not up to making a complete dolls' house yourself, you may surprise yourself with the skills you gain as a miniaturist. I made the 1950s-inspired vases shown overleaf using air-drying clay. You may be able to make your own furniture and furnishings to go inside a shop-bought house.

Commissioning a house from a miniature maker is an alternative, albeit a costly one. The benefit is getting a house that is exactly as you want it. It's the perfect choice for someone who wishes a precise miniature replica of a building with special associations, such as a childhood home. It can be constructed to whatever scale you wish, incorporating details of your choice – such as fireplaces, chimneys, doors and windows.

I made this simple wartime backyard using plans from a dolls' house book. There are many books available containing plans for dolls' houses, miniature shops and other miniature structures.

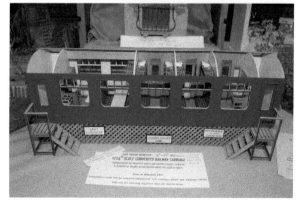

This unusual 24th-scale railway carriage miniature scene was created to be built on a course run by respected miniaturist Jane Harrop.

These 1950s-style 'Zambesi' vases were made using air-dray clay and a felt-tip pen! The scaled-down wallpaper came from a dolls' house 'printies' website, the picture is vintage (possibly Lundby) and the table is from the Dolls House Emporium.

Val Lennie, owner of this dolls' house, wished to recreate a scale model of her childhood home in the picturesque Oxfordshire village of East Hendred. The Stores is a half-timbered Tudor house with herringbone brickwork. She commissioned James Hemsley of Oxfordshire-based Trigger Pond Miniatures to bring her memories to life.

This cabinet house was commissioned, allowing the owner to specify the layout and finishes of her choice.

Room Boxes and Alternatives

Dolls' house collectors do not necessarily collect just houses. Many other buildings are available. Shops are a favourite, because they offer considerable scope for creativity.

A wide range of dolls' 'houses' can be found: churches, beauty parlours, windmills, beach huts, hotels, cafes, railway carriages, caravans … the only limit is imagination.

Room boxes are a great alternative (or supplement) for miniaturists, as they are smaller and easier to accommodate; more affordable; and faster to complete.

Room boxes can be bought as shells (just a box); as a box ready to receive furniture (painted and decorated, lit and often with features such as cornices and ceiling roses); or they can be purchased as simple kits. I made the Wedgwood room box on page 61 using a kit, then personalised it by adding a homemade plinth and pediment.

They are also easy to make from scratch. I made the 'open'-style miniature American diner room box on page 61 from MDF as a reminder of a trip along Route 66 in the United States.

Room boxes need not be plain, pared-down boxes. Some are elaborate and grandiose creations, as the one shown at the top of page 62 – a recreation of a room in the Palace of Versailles – demonstrates.

Unusual containers may also serve as 'room' settings. I have seen a wide variety of items used to house a room scene, including clock cases, cut-away coffee pots, guitars and old radio cases. This works best when there is an association between the container and the scene, such as a café in a coffee pot, or a miniature clock shop in a clock case.

Shadow boxes are like room boxes, only more shallow. They can be wall-mounted, allowing a large collection to be accommodated even in a small full-size house or flat. I used a ready-made shadow box from IKEA to create an attic scene (see page 62, bottom).

Little vignettes offer yet another opportunity to create a small-scale miniature scene. A base of some sort, sometimes with a rear wall, side wall(s) or some other backdrop, can create an evocative scene.

Façades are a great space-saver for the miniaturist. They are effectively dolls' house fronts, without the bulky rooms behind – making them even more slender than a shadow box. They can be hung on walls, and are the perfect collecting choice for lovers of architecture. A façade may comprise the entire front of a building, or just a part, such as a doorway. I have a small collection of doorways, attractively displayed on various walls throughout the house, alongside paintings and framed prints.

Collectors love shops because they can be stocked with anything – hats, lingerie, sweets, groceries, hardware, toys … the scope is endless.

Above: This shop is in the collection of A World in Miniature. A shop can offer great scope, and can be modern or, as here, traditional.

Left: This church kit by Barbara's Mouldings, currently under construction, shows that you don't need to limit yourself to houses.

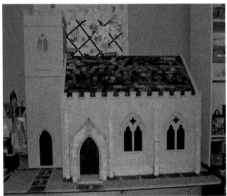

Caravans and other scale models are popular with dolls' house collectors.

This German pier is an unusual miniature.

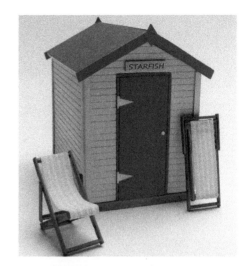

Unusual structures are available in many scales. This beach hut kit by Jane Harrop is a tiny quarter-scale model.

I bought this room box ready-made, decorated and lit. It was made by Anglia Dolls' Houses. All I had to do was add the furniture.

This unusual open-style room box (with sides but no ceiling or front) is made by expert miniaturist Gale Elena Bantock.

This exquisite room box is on display at the World in Miniature Museum at Carlisle. A room box can be a good way to display a small collection on a theme; in this case, musical instruments.

This Chinoiserie room box at the World in Miniature Museum, Carlisle, showcases a collection of beautiful furniture.

This room box by Gale Elena Bantock is in a small cabinet. She sells her room boxes fully decorated, furnished, lit and usually with one or more beautiful figures inside.

This room box by Gale Elena Bantock is open, with no ceiling or front. Such a layout is relatively easy for a novice to make, and commercially made details such as skirting boards and panelling can be used to give a simple form a more sophisticated appearance.

This Gale Elena Bantock model shows that room boxes need not be box-shaped.

This flat-pack room box kit came from the Dolls House Emporium. It was 'pimped' up with the addition of gilded mouldings, Wedgwood medallions, a chimney breast and cornicing.

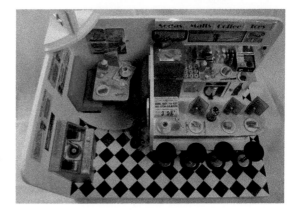

I designed and made this simple 'open'-style room box using MDF, panel pins and wood glue. It is based on an American diner in Albuquerque.

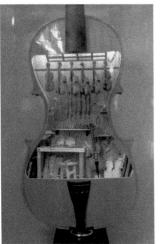

Above: Internationally renowned miniaturist model-makers Mulvaney and Rogers made this room box, the French Room, for A World in Miniature Museum in Carlisle. Trained as art historians, their work is stunning. This is a copy of one of the rooms at the Palace of Versailles near Paris. It has floor-to-ceiling French windows with detailed brass locks and window furniture, and the gilded mouldings are finely crafted and realistic.

Left: Room boxes can be housed in unlikely receptacles, such as this violin shop inside an old violin.

This shadow box was bought from IKEA, and I created the attic scene within it. The idea came from a magazine article, which I adapted to suit my box. Shadow boxes are a good way for miniaturists with smaller homes to build up a wide range of different displays, something that would be impossible with larger dolls' houses.

This shadow box was made by Gale Elena Bantock. The model is quite shallow, but it has the appearance of depth.

These French-style miniatures are made by an Italian maker and combine the shadow-box idea with a façade.

This home made shadow box was made by enthusiast Sheri Followay.

This lovely vignette was created by miniaturist Gale Elena Bantock. It shows how a baseboard and back wall can be used to very good effect.

This Gale Elena Bantock vignette shows how nothing more than a baseboard is required to create a very characterful vignette.

It is essential to pay great attention to detail when creating a vignette, as you can see from this one made by Gale Elena Bantock.

This Gale Elena Bantock vignette shows that there's no need to include figures in a vignette for it to look convincing.

Façades take up little space and offer a good supplement or alternative to a dolls' house collection.

This highly detailed façade is on display in the small museum that forms part of Maple Street dolls' house shop in Hertfordshire.

Even if you don't have the skills or tools to make a complete dolls' house, tackling a wall façade is less daunting. Master miniaturists Mulvany and Rogers, the highly acclaimed bespoke model-makers, occasionally run practical workshops covering a range of useful skills for the amateur miniaturist. One of their short courses involves creating a beautiful wall-hanging Georgian doorway. Tickhill also run frequent courses, including doorways. You could go on to create a whole street of doorways covering different architectural eras.

This door façade was made on a course at Tickhill Dollshouse Courses.

This Greek doorway façade works well in a collection with other doorways of the world.

Collecting Miniatures

Not everyone has space for bulky dolls' houses, but even the most bijou residence can accommodate a miniature collection of some sort. I have full-size blue-and-white Spode china displayed in a large dresser and on wall-mounted display shelves. You may not have space in your kitchen for huge soup tureens and casseroles, but miniature china is so tiny that there's bound to be somewhere you can display it.

Miniature collections can include chairs, hats, musical instruments, silverware, toys, and dressed mannequins. Just collect something you like, and find a way to display your collection attractively.

Above and below: Miniature collections can easily be accommodated in the smallest of spaces, such as my collection of blue-and-white plates on a miniature dresser.

Chairs are a good item to build a miniature collection around, as so many designs are available. This charming chair is in the collection of A World in Miniature, Carlisle.

Miniature paintings are another good collecting area. Collect famous artists, or commission views of local scenes. Invest in attractive frames to showcase your collection.

Miniature collections can be displayed in a room box, as seen here at the World in Miniature Museum.

Diminutive dresses and even tiny shoes and other fashion accessories are keenly collected. This exquisite 12th-scale dress is by American maker Lauren George.

Some collectors have extensive collections of miniature books, displayed in miniature libraries or on tiny bookshelves.

Where to buy

There are plenty of suppliers for miniature collectors looking for brand new dolls' houses and furniture in contemporary and historical styles. The leading online retailer is Dolls House Emporium, who sell dolls' houses and kits, furniture and building materials. There are also many other smaller suppliers and specialist online retailers, as well as artisan makers who sell via the internet. There are British and overseas suppliers, so you will be spoilt for choice.

Big cities also have dolls' house shops, although the number appears to be reducing and many lovely shops have closed over the years. The biggest, and it also has an online presence, is Maple Street in Hertfordshire. Established over two decades ago, they sell one-off handmade items as well as cheaper, mass-produced goods. They also have a stunning onsite dolls' house museum.

Companies such as Dolls House Emporium stock affordable mass-produced miniature furniture and houses.

Some online traders such as Unique Miniatures also sell at dolls' house fairs.

This model of television's famous *Coronation Street* pub is one of many excellent exhibits at Maple Street's museum.

Dolls' house fairs are a fun place to shop. These are held in various cities throughout the year and they offer an opportunity to pick up regional specialities and unusual items from part-time makers who may not sell through any other outlet. Details of forthcoming fairs can be found in dolls' house magazines. In the UK these are: Dolls' House and Miniature Scene Magazine, The Dolls' House Magazine, and Dolls' House World.

Miniatura, the principal dolls' house fair, is held twice annually at the NEC in Birmingham – usually around March and October. It attracts artisan makers as well as sellers of mass-produced items. Although traders are mainly UK-based, the fair attracts stallholders from many parts of the world, so you may find things that are a bit different. Interesting workshops and displays form part of the event.

The Kensington Dolls' House Festival (formerly the London Dollshouse Festival) was established in 1985 and is now one of the top international shows for quality miniatures, with over 175 craftspeople exhibiting, many from abroad. Around 95 per cent of all the items on sale are handmade.

The York Dolls' House and Miniature Fair is held twice annually at York racecourse, attracting over eighty exhibitors.

The Edinburgh Fair is the only remaining dolls' house fair in Scotland, and is held twice every year, in April and November.

There are many fairs across Europe and the United States, if you are lucky enough to time your holiday to coincide with an event. The Andalusia Fair near Malaga is a nice one to attend.

This fair in Scotland offers regional specialities such as miniature haggis and neeps, whisky, and (shown here) some Scottish publications.

Get details of dolls' house shops, fairs and retailers by consulting one of the dolls' house magazines available at newsagents.

One of the many stalls at the bi-annual Miniatura dolls' house and miniatures fair in Birmingham.

Above: Miniature-light-maker Ray Storey showcasing his work at Miniatura.

Left: One of the stalls at the Edinburgh Fair, selling unique dolls' houses.

The Andalusia Fair is held annually and attracts not just Spanish exhibitors, but sellers from other parts of Europe too.

A good place to find dolls' houses – nearly new, second-hand, vintage and occasionally antique – is on second-hand trading websites such as Gumtree and Preloved. You may even pick up a bargain. Such sites offer an affordable way of building up a collection of second-hand houses, making them ideal for anyone wishing to stretch their budget or put their own stamp on a tatty property by refurbishing it to their own taste. Vintage, second-hand, new and antique dolls' houses and accessories can be bought through online auction sites too, such as eBay.

There are also specialist second-hand dolls' house outlets online, some operated by enthusiasts offering parts of their excess collections for sale via various dolls' house blogs. Specialist sites are a particularly useful hunting ground when searching for a specific model. Some also trade in vintage spares too, so if you have a window or door missing or damaged, you may find a suitable replacement.

Antique shops and auctions are another source, especially for older properties and for vintage furniture. Generally auctions are cheaper than antique shops, as an auction house is the equivalent of buying wholesale and an antique shop or centre will charge retail prices. However, always remember that an auction house will charge you a commission on the hammer price of around 10–15 per cent.

Some miniaturists use the website Etsy to look for things they can't find anywhere else. Etsy is a marketplace where creative entrepreneurs around the world connect to make and sell unique goods. Dolls' houses, room boxes, furniture and accessories – new and vintage – can be found on Etsy.

Occasional swap shops sometimes take place at dolls' house clubs, offering yet another opportunity to secure miniature items.

You will find that you most likely use a mixture of different outlets, depending on the item you are looking for.

This unusual continental miniature shop and contents, *c.* 1890, with textured cork façade and sides, was sold by Bonhams. That auction house ceased its toy and doll sales in 2015, but other auctioneers do have specialist dolls' house sales from time to time.

Protecting, Displaying and Renovating your Collection

Having invested time, effort and money in buying or making a dolls' house, or amassing a collection of miniatures, take care of it and display it to best effect.

Protection

Small items are dust magnets. If you have a collection of, say, miniature shoes, or chairs, or other tiny treasures, keep them behind glass if you can – such as in a glass cabinet, display case or glazed shadow box or room box. This is not always possible, especially if your collection includes a larger item such as a dolls' house. Dusting will be an inevitable part of your care and protection ritual. A soft feature duster is the best implement for a dolls' house, but take care around fragile parts of the house – such as finials and weather vanes. You don't want to damage anything. Blowing to dislodge dust from hard-to-reach crevices works for me, but try not to breathe it in if you have a dust allergy! A small, soft artist's paint brush is effective inside a dolls' house for reaching into corners and for dusting items of miniature furniture. Small battery-operated vacuum cleaners designed for computer keyboards can also be useful tools.

Dust carefully, especially inside your dolls' house where there may be fragile pieces of furniture. Try a small artist's paintbrush to dislodge dust.

Aesthetic considerations may be a primary driver when you decide where to place your collection within your home: obviously a dolls' house needs to be displayed where it will look great. But remember practical matters too. You don't want anyone bashing against it and causing damage, so steer clear of high-traffic areas such as hallways, landings and near doorways. Anywhere with wide temperature fluctuations can also pose problems, as wood will expand and contract in response to hot and cold, potentially causing cracking and splitting. Avoid conservatories, which can get hot during the day when the sun is out, but very cold at night. The same goes for anywhere too close to a radiator. Sunny window sills are another no-no, as paint and paper may fade or peel in the heat and strong light.

Much as we love our pets and children, they can be both boisterous and curious – a dangerous combination where miniatures are concerned. Not only might they damage your treasures, but your miniatures might harm them, so remember that small items are choking hazards.

Display

A 12th-scale house is large and, being made of MDF or ply, is very heavy. You will need a sturdy piece of furniture such as a table or chest of drawers upon which to display one. Mass-produced and custom-made dolls' house stands are available too.

A 24th-scale cottage is easier to display, as it will fit neatly onto a small side table, taking up the same footprint as a few books.

Smaller scale houses, such as quarter scale, are lighter in weight and take up less space, so they will fit onto a small shelf or even on a wall.

Walls tend to be under-exploited by miniaturists, yet they provide ample space for spectacular displays of collections of miniature items. Walls are the perfect place for all manner of miniatures, but they work best with displays that do not project too much, such as the two-dimensional façade of a building rather than a three-dimensional deep dolls' house. I have an old printers' tray (originally used to store their printing blocks). It's the perfect display case for all of those bits and pieces picked up at dolls' house fairs, which have yet to find a permanent home.

This English early-nineteenth-century dolls' house, sold by Bonhams, looks very fine on its original three-drawer stand. Dolls' houses look good displayed on a chest of drawers or table painted to blend with the dolls' house's colour scheme.

Dolls' house stands in 12th scale can be bought in kit form and easily assembled at home. This one is from Barbara's Mouldings.

This early wooden castellated Gothic dolls' house, English and circa 1830, sits on a late-seventeenth-century-style carved pine stand with S-scroll supports, a central floral cartouche and swag chains. It shows that the stand can be as beautiful as the dolls' house.

A 24th-scale model can often fit neatly onto a coffee table, along with other objects such as books.

This tiny 48th-scale dolls' house, a kit made by Petite Properties and customised by Gale Elena Bantock, sits on a diminutive chest of drawers. The house is now in a private collection in Japan.

This 48th-scale Petite Properties kit is the same as the one shown above, but this time personalised by quarter-scale enthusiast Heather Drinkwater and placed on a plinth.

Display miniature collections to great effect in a vintage printers' tray.

Right: A Stokesay Ware bread pan in the pigeon hole of a printers' tray.

Below: 12th-scale Stokesay Ware jars and a miniature ewer and jug on display in a printers' tray.

You may have overlooked acres of under-exploited display space staring you in the face: your walls. This 48th-scale house by Gale Elena Bantock, now with a collector in the United States, fits easily on a wall.

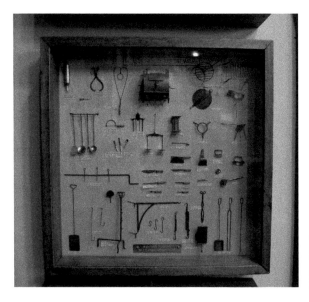

This framed collection of miniature household metalware in a case in a Los Angeles museum is both decorative and interesting.

Wall-brackets provide another solution to the perennial display space shortage. They are suitable only for out-of-the-way positions – high up, or in a quiet spot without too many passers-by to knock against them – but the benefit is that they create valuable space for items with a larger footprint, such as small dolls' houses. Wall brackets are especially suited to the display of 24th-scale buildings and shallow 12th-scale houses. Just attach a simple but strong bracket to your wall, taking care to ensure that your walls are sturdy enough to take the weight. By hanging it from a wall, you conserve surface space on your furniture for your larger dolls' houses.

Use the same technique but with a high-level shelf running around the top of your room. This can look really dramatic and it's a fabulous way to keep your treasured dolls' houses away from curious little hands and careless pets! However, the dusting can present some challenges – although arguably it's harder to see dust so high up! Again, be sure to check that the shelf is well anchored to the wall, as you wouldn't want it to come crashing down and smashing your precious houses to smithereens – or, worse, injuring someone. So if you're going up the wall looking for somewhere to accommodate your growing collection, take a look at your wallspace.

Shelves and brackets around a room can create valuable space for displaying small or lightweight dolls' houses.

Renovating and Conserving

Antique dolls' houses are best left as they are, to preserve their character and value. If you can afford to, buy houses that are in good internal and external condition. They will hold their value, retain their desirability, and look more authentic.

With a vintage house, you may need to consider whether to restore/renovate (put back features such as missing windows, and repaint worn surfaces, to bring a house back it its original, new condition); to preserve (making minimal or no changes to your vintage house, but stabilising it to prevent deterioration and using original items where changes are necessary); or to conserve (keep in as unaltered a condition as possible, with any repairs or additions fully reversible and removable without the condition of the original house being altered). Repairs and alterations to a vintage house should be sympathetic, so as not to damage its charm and character, or its future value.

Most collectors prefer vintage houses in original condition – even if a tad playworn. However, sometimes a house can benefit from sympathetic restoration if it is too far gone to be displayable – such as those which have been stored in sheds, and have water damage and mold. Use old adverts, catalogues and photographs available online to help you ensure your handiwork is authentic to the original. If you're lucky, you may even find the original plans that were used to build your vintage dolls' house.

You may find that a window or door is missing from your vintage house. Replacing it with a period original can enhance the look and value of your dolls' house. Vintage spares are available online. The tin windows and doors pictured on page 86 are made by Romside. Romside made metal windows, doors, shutters, awnings, porches, stairs, fireplaces and chimney stacks with pots. Their components were used by several manufacturers of dolls' houses, such as Gee Bee, over many years. They were also available individually through Hobbies for self-build, so many shed-built dolls' houses produced by fathers across the land will have Romside doors and windows. They also fitted the plans for dolls' houses that Hobbies sold. The ones pictured on page 86 look very similar to windows made by Tri-ang.

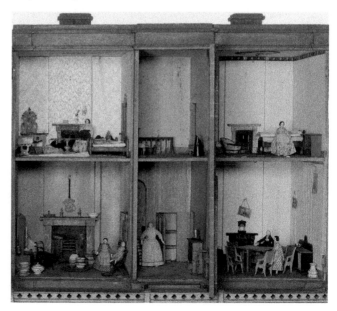

This early nineteenth-century English dolls' house has faded wallpaper, which is wrinkled in places. Stripping it out and replacing it would destroy its charm – and its value!

The painted wooden dolls' house on the left (English, circa 1880) is in good condition. The one on the right has a red-brick lithographed front in good condition, but the windows are missing. These could be replaced, or the house could be left as it is.

Left: This antique dolls' house is in great condition externally. Look for damage when buying an old house, and use your nose too – they can sometimes be rather musty if left languishing, unloved, in a damp outhouse!

Below: Images from old catalogues can be used to ensure an authentic restoration of your vintage dolls' house.

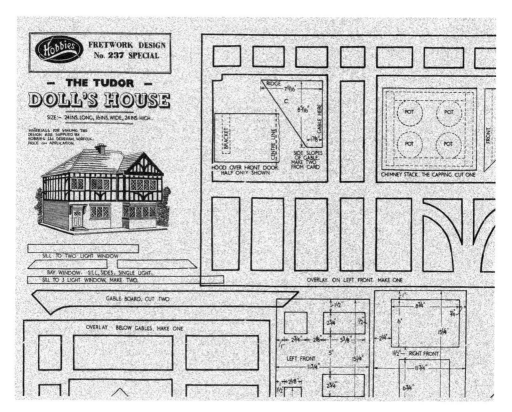

Above: One lucky owner of a vintage house managed to buy plans from the internet upon which her dolls' house was based. Such plans are collectable in their own right, as well as being a good source material.

Right: Try entering the name/model of your dolls' house into a search engine and see what source material is available to help you recreate details with accuracy.

Images can be found on websites run by dolls' house enthusiasts.

Original doors, windows and other vintage components are available online, such as these Romside components.

This Romside fireplace is fitted in a
vintage Hobbies house.

Where to See Miniatures

There are many miniature collections across the world, too many to feature here. This is just a small selection of some of the best.

United Kingdom

Queen Mary's Dolls' House, Windsor

Created for Queen Mary by the leading British architect, Sir Edwin Lutyens, between 1921 and 1924, this spectacular 12th-scale house has thousands of objects made by leading artists, designers and craftsmen. Famous for having electricity, running hot and cold water, working lifts and flushing lavatories, this miniature home really is fit for a queen.

Windsor Castle, Windsor, Berkshire SL4 1NJ www.royalcollection.org.uk

Victoria and Albert Museum of Childhood, London

The Museum holds around 100 dolls' houses, models and shops. The earliest is the Nuremberg house of 1673; one of the most recent, the twenty-first-century Kaleidoscope house. There is also a baby house, The Tate, dating back to 1760.

V&A Museum of Childhood, Cambridge Heath Road, London E2 9PA www.vam.ac.uk

The famous Peggy Lines house is on display at the museum. Inside, original Tri-ang furniture includes their kit-made Queen Anne range. The pink bedroom has a Westacre Village suite comprising four-poster bed, ottoman, armchairs and sofa. Other furniture commissioned for the house includes a wooden dressing table, wardrobes, beds, chest, dining room cupboard, writing desk with upper book shelves, side boards, table with matching chairs and upholstered chairs. Some of the furniture was made by Elgin Ltd of Enfield.

A World in Miniature Museum, Carlisle

Quality miniatures, from copies of antique furniture, paintings and china in beautiful room settings to everyday items at 12th scale, form the collection. Made with skill and craftsmanship and attractively displayed, the museum is perfect for enthusiasts. They even have the world's smallest teddy bear!

A World in Miniature Museum, Houghton Hall Garden Centre, Carlisle, Cumbria, CA6 4JB www.aworldinminiature.com

Museum of Childhood, Edinburgh

The world's first museum of childhood, founded in 1955, has five floors of childhood memorabilia, including antique dolls, dolls' houses and miniature shops. The English butcher's shop, dating from the 1880s, even has a royal warrant. The collection also contains a couple of English open-fronted grocers' shops dating from the late nineteenth century, plus miniature properties from America, Peru and Germany.

Museum of Childhood, 42 High Street, Royal Mile, Edinburgh EH1 1TG
www.edinburghmuseums.org.uk/venues/museum-of-childhood

Newby Hall, Yorkshire

For over forty years, friends Caroline Hamilton and Jane Fiddick have shared a passion for dolls' houses. Their collection is now housed at Newby Hall and includes nearly seventy houses of all shapes, sizes, styles and ages. It is one of the most important private collections on display anywhere in the world. The collection ranges from small room boxes such as Grandmama's Parlour to the grand Beagle House. There are Victorian shops, rustic family homes, architectural classics and even a yuppie bachelor pad!

Newby Hall and Gardens, Ripon, North Yorkshire, HG4 5AE www.newbyhall.com

This pretty Victorian bedroom is one of the many 12th-scale room boxes on display in Carlisle.

English butcher's shop from the 1880s, at the Museum of Childhood, Edinburgh. Joints of meat are temptingly displayed on a well-stacked table outside, and gruesome carcasses hang from meat hooks. Two portly hand-carved wooden butchers complete the scene.

Babbacombe Model Village, Devon

This outdoor model village opened in 1963 on a four-acre site near Torquay, set in beautiful miniature landscaped gardens. It has over 400 12th-scale buildings and over 1,000 feet of model railway track. There are buildings of every type and era. Perhaps the 'oldest' is the scaled-down Stonehenge, a perfect copy of the historic attraction on Salisbury Plain. There's also a castle, zoo, mini medieval mansion house, village cricket scene, and even modern architecture, including a wind farm and a housing estate.

Babbacombe Model Village, Hampton Avenue, Babbacombe, Torquay, Devon TQ1 3LA www.babbacombemodelvillage.co.uk

Babbacombe has many picturesque model houses, shops and other buildings.

Wimborne Minster Model Village, Dorset

This is a 10th-scale reproduction of the actual town of Wimborne Minster as it was in the 1950s, with over 300 models including 100-plus shops – luggage shops, jewellers, wool shops, greengrocers, post office, gents' outfitters, shoe shops, drapers, bakeries, toy and sweet shops, chemists, cycle shops, car showroom, coke and coal merchant, hairdressers and barbers, watchmakers, opticians, a charming television and radio shop with a Bush 'box' television in the window, a branch of Woolworths ... plus pubs and banks. From the miniature public toilets comes the distinctive sound of flushing WCs! The red phone box emits a ringing sound. The organ can be heard playing in the Minster, where a wedding is taking place. Listen to the church bells chime on the hour.

16 King Street, Wimborne Minster, Dorset, BH21 1DY www.wimborne-modeltown. com

Wallington, Morpeth

The dolls' house room at Wallington has eighteen houses on display. Hammond House is the jewel of the collection, with thirty-six fully furnished rooms and 1,500 pieces of furniture, it dates to 1880–99. It has electric lights in every room and even used to have running water.

Cambo, near Morpeth, Northumberland, NE61 4AR www.nationaltrust.org.uk

Wallington is run by the National Trust, who have many other dolls' houses in their collection. These include: an eighteenth-century dolls' house at Nostell Priory, Yorkshire, full of elaborately crafted miniature furniture, including tiny Chippendale pieces; an eighteenth-century dolls' house and contents at Uppark House, Sussex; Beatrix Potter's dolls' house at Hill Top, Cumbria, which inspired 'The Tale of Two Bad Mice'; and an eighteenth-century baby house and series of miniature rooms (part of the Carlisle Collection of miniature period rooms brought from Greys Court, Henley in 1981) at Nunnington Hall, Yorkshire.

One of the dolls' houses that can be seen at the National Trust's Wallington. (National Trust Images/ Andreas von Einsiedel)

The 'Queen Anne Drawing Room' is part of the Carlisle Collection of miniature rooms on display at the National Trust's Nunnington Hall. (National Trust Images/Mike Williams)

Europe

Netherlands

Madurodam
Opened in 1952, Madurodam is a 1:25-scale city covering an area of 18,000m². It comprises six motorways and eight waterways; a beach and harbour; oil refinery and natural gas plant; container port, international airport and railway stations; a 6,000-seater

Madurodam is near The Hague in the Netherlands.

stadium, gardens and parade grounds; a Parliament, department stores, office blocks and factories; churches and a synagogue; monuments, statues, public squares and street cafes; civic buildings and historic homes – plus 66,000 multi-racial inhabitants. Madurodam's railways cover over 4 km and comprise over 80,000 tiny railway sleepers.

Madurodam, 1 George Maduroplein, 2584 RZ Den Haag, Netherlands www.madurodam.nl

Germany

Nuremberg Toy Museum (Spielzeugmuseum)
Opened in 1971, the museum's four floors contain historic toys. On the first floor, dolls and dolls' houses allow a glimpse of life in centuries past. The earliest surviving dolls' house, dating back to 1611, is in the nearby German National Museum (Germanisches Nationalmuseum at Kartäusergasse 1), along with other early dolls' houses.

Toy Museum (Museum Lydia Bayer), Karlstraße 13-15, 90403 Nuremberg www.museums.nuremberg.de/toy-museum

Sweden

Nordiska Museet, Stockholm
Housed in Sweden's beautiful equivalent to the V&A on Djurgarden, one of Stockholm's many islands, is a collection of fifteen dolls' houses spanning three centuries. Tucked away near the top of the museum, most of the 'houses' are in fact cabinets kitted out as dolls' houses. Dating from 1700 to 1992, the collection is mainly eighteenth- and nineteenth-century, with one house from the 1930s and one from 1992. The 1936 house has a lift connecting the four floors, and a 1930s motor parked in the garage.

Djurgårdsvägen 6–16, Djurgården, Stockholm www.nordiskamuseet.se

United States

Art Institute of Chicago
The Thorne Rooms, a priceless collection of sixty-eight of the world's finest room boxes, can be found here. Created by Narcissa Niblack Thorne, a wealthy woman, she created employment during the Great Depression by hiring talented craftspeople to work on miniature rooms. A permanent gallery was established for the Thorne rooms at the Art Institute in 1954. The rooms, mainly American, English and French, are exquisite and well worth a visit.

Art Institute of Chicago, 111 South Michigan Avenue, Chicago www.artic.edu/aic/collections/thorne

Museum of Science and Industry, Chicago
This is not a miniatures museum, but it does have a special dolls' house on display – the Fairy Castle, a miniature chateau (although at nearly 9 feet square and up to 12 feet tall in places, this is not a bijoux building). Created by Hollywood star Colleen Moore, its opulent interiors feature over 2,000 quality miniature items: antique vases;

Exhibits being prepared for display at the Miniature Museum of Greater St Louis.

gold and diamond chandeliers; 500-year-old rose quartz and carved jade items from the Chinese royal collection; and original artworks. Attention to detail includes a convincing miniature 'bear skin' rug, made by a taxidermist from an ermine pelt, with perfectly in-scale teeth from a mouse!

The Museum of Science and Industry, 5700 S. Lake Shore Drive, Chicago, IL 60637 www.msichicago.org/whats-here/exhibits/fairycastle

Angels Attic, Santa Monica
Founded in 1984 and owned by millionaire dolls' house enthusiast Jackie McMahan, this private museum is housed in a traditional Victorian house a short walk from Santa Monica pier. The varied collection includes: a Boer War house, a London town house carved from a wooden apple crate by a sailor; an unusual boot-shaped miniature house based on the rhyme of the old lady who lived in a shoe; the *Heidi* room box, believed to have once belonged to Johanna Spyri, author of *Heidi*; and a spectacular Palace of Versailles created by master British makers Mulvany and Rogers.

Angels Attic, 516 Colorado Avenue, Santa Monica, California www.angelsattic.com

Miniature Museum of Greater St Louis
Founded in 1989, this private museum is a three-storey 11,000-foot former store filled with dolls' houses and miniatures of every size, style and era. There are exhibits everywhere – even in the museum's toilets! This well-stocked museum contains a shopping centre, cathedral, windmill, shops, diminutive gardens, swimming pools and ponds, a four-storey apartment, farmhouses and barns, a doctor's surgery, 1950s ice-cream parlour, barber shop, jail, a scene from an opera, a playboy's penthouse … and much more, all in miniature.

Miniature Museum of Greater St Louis, 4746 Gravois Avenue, St. Louis, MO 63116 www.miniaturemuseum.org

Above: Angels Attic dolls' house museum in California is full of many fine exhibits.

Right: One of the many houses on display in St Louis.